Narcissism

A Comprehensive Manual For Overcoming And
Neutralizing The Covert Aggressive Narcissist
In Your Personal Sphere, Reclaim Your
Personal Empowerment And Achieve
Emotional Healing From A Harmful
Relationship

Jean-Pierre Trudeau

TABLE OF CONTENT

Cultural Importance 1

Seven Narcissistic Types 8

Relationships: The Role Of Effective Communication 23

Narcissism: Overt And Covered 38

Getting Past Grief 62

The Narcissistic Mind's Inner Workings 77

Protect The Limits You've Selected To Establish 88

The Culture And Narcissism 105

Cultural Importance

Let's examine how these stories from Egyptian, Chinese, and Indian mythology have influenced societal views on narcissism.

Indian Mythology and Narcissism: The Cultural Significance of Ramayana's Ravana

In India and elsewhere, the character of Ravana has had a significant influence on societal attitudes towards narcissism. Here are some significant influencing points:

Moral guidance: The story of Ravana serves as a warning about the disastrous effects of unbridled ego and desire. His narrative serves as a helpful reminder of the need for modesty and deference to others' personal space.

Moral conundrums: Ravana's persona brings up moral concerns around consent, desire, and the misuse of authority. Talks concerning the limits of love and the repercussions of following one's desires at the expense of others are sparked by his acts.

Literary and creative influence: Indian theatre, art, and literature have frequently featured Ravana's persona. Writers and artists frequently use him to explore the complexity of human nature by serving as a symbol of conceit and haughtiness.

Chinese Mythology's Narcissism—Xi Shi: Cultural Significance

The narrative of Xi Shi has had a long-lasting influence on Chinese society and narcissistic beliefs:

Xi Shi's story highlights the attraction of physical beauty and how it can mislead others. Beauty and vanity. It has influenced conversations on how important appearance is in Chinese culture.

Icons of culture: In Chinese culture, Xi Shi is revered as representing femininity and beauty. She is now a cultural figure since so many poems, paintings, and other creative works have been influenced by her story.

Tale of caution: Xi Shi uses her experience to warn others about the perils of extreme self-absorption and its negative effects on society. It promotes contemplation on the repercussions of putting one's conceit ahead of the larger good.

Egyptian Mythology's Narcissism—The Cultural Significance of the Pharaohs

The following are some ways that the alleged narcissism of the Pharaohs has shaped cultural perceptions:

Royal authority: The social structure of ancient Egypt was formed by the Pharaohs' conviction in their divine position, which strengthened the notion of absolute royal authority.

Architectural legacy: The Pharaohs' infatuation with imposing architecture profoundly impacted Egyptian culture. Specifically, the pyramids represent their magnificence and faith in their enduring legacy.

From a historical perspective: The actions of the Pharaohs provide historical context for understanding the connection between kings, power, and self-aggrandizement. Their experiences have sparked ongoing conversations on humility, leadership, and legacy.

The stories from Egyptian, Chinese, and Indian mythology have greatly influenced how people view narcissism in society. They offer insightful information about the negative effects of excessive self-love and the value of harmony, modesty, and respect in interpersonal interactions and social systems. These tales are still relevant today because they provoke thought about the intricacies of human nature and the pervasiveness of narcissism in our daily lives.

Typical Characters

Let us first define narcissistic archetypal personalities before discussing their traits and social ramifications.

Describe the archetypal narcissistic characters: A subset of fictional or actual people that represent the archetype of Narcissus—a Greek mythological figure famed for his extreme self-love and vanity—are known as narcissistic archetypal characters. These characters frequently exhibit a group of characteristics and actions that are indicative of narcissistic tendencies. They are common in real-world settings, books, movies, and TV series.

Recognizing recurrent qualities in characters:

Overindulgence in oneself: Narcissistic personalities frequently exhibit an exaggerated feeling of their significance. They think that, in some manner, they are different from others and better.

Lack of empathy: They frequently show a marked absence of empathy for others. They find it difficult to relate to or comprehend the needs and feelings of others around them.

Manipulative behavior: In order to forward their agendas, narcissistic individuals may take advantage of and manipulate others. They frequently see others as instruments to further their agendas.

The constant need for approval: They want other people's approval and affirmation. Their need for continuous attention stems from their reliance on outside validation for their self-worth.

Feeling of entitlement: Narcissistic individuals think they are entitled to preferential treatment and benefits. They may not even have to work for what they feel entitled to.

Fragile self-esteem: Ironically, weak self-esteem hides behind their confident front. They react angrily or defensively to criticism because they are extremely sensitive.

Relationship difficulties: Because of their narcissistic inclinations, it is difficult for them to establish and preserve meaningful, healthy relationships. When someone no longer serves their interests, they could use and discard them.

Delusions of influence and power: Grandiose delusions of influence, power, and success are frequently held by narcissistic individuals. These fantasies fuel their need for dominance.

Shallow emotional depth: They could find it difficult to establish a strong emotional bond with other people. They frequently exhibit petty and self-serving feelings.

Seven Narcissistic Types

It is important to be aware of the following seven sorts of narcissists: the exhibitionist, the sexual, the hyper-vigilant, the classic, the covert, and the malignant types.

The Traditional NarcissistThe adoration and appreciation of others tends to be the lifeblood of classic narcissists. They typically want to be the center of attention because they feel they are more unique or valuable than others. When it serves their purpose or agenda, they don't mind using others, and they are easily angered when someone tries to deny them something they believe they are entitled to.

The Disguised Narcissist
This kind of narcissist presents as powerless and is often passive-aggressive. People who constantly complain and put themselves in the victim role are seen as covert narcissists. They frequently act like victims and will quickly

create a situation to attract attention. These narcissists experience sadness and worry.

The Overly Watchful Narcissist

Narcissists who are hypervigilant are extremely perceptive to the emotions and tone of others. They are extremely perceptive to other people's tone and body language. They, therefore, take things personally and get hurt quickly when someone criticizes them. Why? Because they are fundamentally self-obliterating while also being afflicted with shame and humiliation. The hyper-vigilant type is the opposite of the exhibitionist or covert narcissist type, who likes being the center of attention. They are likely to act directly towards others and dislike being in the spotlight.

The Narcissistic Oblivious.

Lack of empathy is one of the primary characteristics shared by all narcissists, and the oblivious narcissist has no concept of other people's feelings. They are insensitive to individuals and lack awareness of them. They appear to be without the sensitivity chip. They will, therefore, come across as haughty and hostile. They feel compelled to be the center of attention since they feel the world revolves around them.

The Narcissist Exhibitionist.

Someone superficial and materialistic is an exhibitionist. They enjoy being the center of attention and are conceited. In actuality, they are continuously looking for approval and attention. For this kind of narcissist, it's like an endless hole. Unknowingly, they are the most self-conscious persons in the room despite believing they are superior to everyone else in physical and intellectual abilities. They battle an inferiority complex deep inside. They would become depressed as a result of the overpowering realization of their true state of being. Their insatiable thirst for praise indicates their underlying yearning for acceptance and love.

The narcissistic sexual person.
This kind of narcissist feels so entitled to have their sexual demands satisfied that their need to engage in sexual activity is heightened. They have a limited and selfish perspective on sex. Due to their self-centeredness, they become entitled and have little respect for their partner's emotions or needs. They are self-centered and only consider what is physically necessary for them. They are indifferent and unable to satisfy their partner's craving for closeness. They frequently exaggerate their sexual prowess, yet their performance in the bedroom deserves a lot of recognition. Because

that's what they ultimately perceive it to be: a performance. In general, they respond badly to rejection in the bedroom and put pressure on their partner to engage in sexual activity. They are expert manipulators who can seduce and convince someone to have sex with them. If you don't comply with their sexual demands, they even threaten to have sex with someone else. In order to satisfy their sexual demands, narcissists of this kind would lie and cheat.

The Narcissist with Malice.
The malignant narcissist poses an immediate threat. It is a form of narcissism that those with narcissistic personality disorder (NPD) exhibit. Psychologists also refer to it as antisocial personality disorder. You need to understand that having a narcissistic personality disorder (NPD) diagnosis is not the same as displaying narcissistic behavioral patterns. The pathological narcissist is incapable of empathy.

Because they are violent, angry, paranoid, and sadistic individuals, they are either sociopaths or psychopaths. They treat others like less than human beings and cannot feel regret for hurting someone. Adolf Hitler, according to many psychoanalysts, is a prime example of a malignant narcissist. They are hazardous. They are the most dangerous kind of narcissists by far since they will create suffering on all fronts: psychological, sexual, emotional, financial, and physical. They won't feel guilty or look back on anything they've done.

You'll notice that a common characteristic shared by all of these narcissist types is their inability to be emotionally vulnerable enough to develop a close emotional bond with another person. Though they seem to be there, it feels like they are absent when considering your feelings and paying attention to how you feel. The issues start when they stop being emotionally present. Emotional closeness is as necessary as physical intimacy for a relationship to be healthy and endure a lifetime. Thus, the following queries come to mind. When you realize your partner exhibits traits of one or more of these narcissistic kinds, what should you do? Is it better to stay in the relationship or end it?

In the end, the choice is yours.

Chapter 3: Narcissistic Personality Disorder Treatments

NPD can be extremely difficult to treat even though there are medicines available for those who have it. The majority of therapists discover that the most effective way to treat patients with NPD is to assist them in managing their symptoms. This illness can be challenging to treat in a therapeutic context for several reasons.

Firstly, it is difficult to modify these characteristics since they are deeply embedded in the individual's mentality. This is mostly because most personality features develop during childhood, and behavior begins to form at a very young age. Second, NPD can be very challenging to treat due to its nature. Individuals with this illness think they are more capable, brighter, and deserving of special care than those around them. This implies that they frequently are completely unaware that there is an issue. Typically, someone will only seek therapy if those in their lives deliberately attempt to bring up their problems. Of course, the patient must acknowledge the problem for therapy to be effective.

Additionally, after starting therapy, patients often undervalue their therapist, which makes it challenging to build a therapeutic relationship that enables the patient to relate to the therapist and explore their problem. Families of individuals with NPD may find suggestions for behavior modification in the upcoming chapter of this book. Here are a few of the instruments that psychiatrists use to treat NPD.

Because NPD patients frequently show open disrespect for their physicians or therapists, thinking they are more knowledgeable about what is wrong than the professionals, many psychiatrists and psychologists find it challenging to treat NPD patients. To stop their carers from assisting the patient in changing, they could even attempt to scare them.

For persons with NPD, therapy alternatives are available despite these challenges. Below is a list of these:

Personal Counselling

A therapist works one-on-one with the patient in individual therapy. Narcissistic behaviors initially caused the problem by helping the patient build stronger relationships with others and recognize that others are distinct individuals with their own needs, ideas, and goals. This is usually not a short-term prospect; in order to accomplish all of these objectives, an individual with NPD may need to attend therapy for years. That being said, there's no need to give up. If the patient is open to change and willing to put forth some effort, some changes can happen quickly. The patient's willingness to monitor and adjust their actions when they become intolerable may cause the changes.

For instance, cognitive-behavioral therapy can effectively address the patient's need to learn how to comprehend and control their emotions. One of the initial steps in a therapy session may also involve helping a patient grasp an alternative point of view. The patient can be trained to see when they are going too far and to distinguish their ideas, feelings, and thoughts from those of others.

Helping the patient deal with failure and criticism is another topic that can be discussed in therapy. Being criticized or having anything go wrong for them can be extremely difficult for someone with NPD because they feel they are beyond retaliation. In these situations, they may lash out at people or blame others for their failure. A therapist can assist this person in realizing their errors, motivate them to quit assigning blame, and teach them what to do in the event of failure or criticism. The patient will discover that acting out is not the best way to handle criticism.

Helping a person with NPD perceive and comprehend the emotions of those around them is another area of change that can be addressed in therapy. This includes •Educating the patient to become more aware of their true capabilities and limitations. Therapists can accurately help patients recognize their areas of strength and weakness, their limits, and when they require assistance.

•Teaching them how to take positive feedback.

- Assist the patient with concerns related to their self-worth. Ultimately, a lot of individuals with NPD could present an exaggerated sense of self to the outer world, but on the inside, they might be using this façade to mask low self-esteem.
- The therapist can start exploring the root causes of the patient's narcissism, like childhood trauma if trust has been established in the therapy partnership. The most time and effort will be expended during this portion of therapy.

Group Counselling

For someone with narcissistic personality disorder, group therapy sessions with a therapist are also highly recommended. This provides the individual with a regulated environment to practice successful social interaction. In group therapy, an individual with NPD can practice self-control in social situations, get support from other patients when they act out, and role-play conflicts with a therapist skilled in managing this disease. As a result, the patient will learn how to interact with people more effectively. Under the supervision of other patients who have progressed further in the process, a qualified therapist also helps the patient learn to recognize others as distinct from oneself. The individual with NPD may learn more quickly as a result of this. Additionally, patients who have progressed in their therapy can assist younger patients. People may learn a lot from one another when given the chance.

Drugs

While there are many psychiatric drugs on the market, the majority do not address NPD symptoms directly. Alternatively, medication may be administered to address indirect problems that a person with NPD may experience, like sadness and anxiety (particularly during therapy for issues related to poor self-esteem). Psychotropic drugs, in the opinion of many psychiatrists, are completely ineffective for treating NPD.

Being admitted to a hospital

Severe NPD patients may, in extreme circumstances, be admitted to a mental health facility. This can occur if a person's symptoms are so bad that they endanger themselves or others. People with NPD can be volatile, making it possible that they could put themselves at risk since they may take behaviors too far and find it difficult to distinguish between danger and nothing. Their inability to regulate their impulses may be a factor in risky behavior. Furthermore, they might use their aggression against someone else if they are upset with someone. Once more, their incapacity to restrain their urges may cause them to physically attack other people.

Any hospital stay for NPD should ideally be brief and focused on treating the particular symptom that first brought the patient to the hospital. For those with NPD, long-term hospitalization has not been proven to be beneficial.

Individual and group psychotherapy is the most successful treatment for NPD. When combined, these therapies can aid in the development of more secure relationships and a more realistic self-image for the narcissistic personality disorder sufferer. They can control and change their behavior. They may be able to address their problems more skillfully if they are educated to comprehend the underlying causes of their behavior.

Those who often work with individuals who suffer from NPD will find valuable insights into their behavior and strategies for improving it in the upcoming chapter. There are also tips and methods to assist people in changing their behavior.

Relationships: The Role Of Effective Communication

In order to foster real connections, effective communication is essential, especially while trying to overcome narcissism. It takes more thoughtful, reciprocal, and empathic interaction to replace self-centered communication styles in successful partnerships. In order to create sincere connections, the following are essential guidelines for communicating well in relationships:

1. Put Active Listening Into Practice: An essential component of successful communication is active listening. Take part in the discussion to the fullest, show that you are attentive, and show that you are genuinely interested in what the other person has to say.

2. Use "I" sentences: While expressing your ideas and sentiments, use "I" sentences to avoid being critical. It promotes free communication

and helps to avoid assigning blame. Speak like "I feel" rather than "You always."

3. Pay Attention to Non-Verbal Cues: Non-verbal clues, like body language and facial expressions, are important parts of communication. Pay close attention to these signs to ensure your words and body language are genuine and transparent.

4. Steer Clear of Defensiveness: Overcoming narcissism necessitates controlling defensiveness. Seek to comprehend the other person's viewpoint rather than responding defensively to criticism or opposing views. This opens the door to honest and fruitful communication.

5. Seek Clarification: Seek clarification rather than assuming anything when there is doubt or ambiguity. By doing so, misconceptions that could strain relationships are avoided, and it shows a dedication to understanding the other person's point of view.

6. Show Empathy: Convey empathy into your interactions by acknowledging and respecting the feelings and experiences of the other person. Demonstrating empathy fosters trust and fortifies the emotional bond between partners.

7. Be Brief and Clear: Clear communication is essential to effective communication. Communicate succinctly and directly, letting them know what's on your mind and how you feel. As a result, there is less chance of misunderstanding and a more concentrated conversation.

8. Provide Constructive Feedback: When providing feedback, avoid generic criticism and concentrate on particular, constructive remarks instead. This strategy stimulates constructive change and fosters a collaborative environment.

9. Admit Mistakes and Offer Sincere Apologies: The capacity to admit faults and extend

heartfelt apologies is essential to overcoming narcissism. If you are truly sorry for any mistakes you have made, accept responsibility for them. This encourages trust and shows humility.

10. Promote Open Communication: Establish a setting where both sides feel free to share their ideas and feelings to promote open communication. This transparency adds to the relationship's genuineness and depth.

11. Select the Appropriate Time: Consider when you will be communicating. To have a meaningful discussion, pick times when you and the other person are both emotionally accessible and responsive. When things are tense, steer clear of talking about delicate subjects.

12. Celebrate Success Together: Part of effective communication is getting together to celebrate successes. Celebrate one other's victories and express your gratitude to each

other. This encouraging feedback helps to create a helpful relationship by solidifying the link.

To foster real connections and overcome narcissism, effective communication is essential. Individuals can foster relationships marked by understanding, empathy, and authenticity through the use of "I" statements, active listening, being aware of non-verbal cues, avoiding defensiveness, asking clarifying questions, expressing empathy, being succinct, providing constructive feedback, admitting mistakes, promoting open communication, selecting the appropriate time, and jointly celebrating successes.

Gradually Ending A Negative Relationship

In a perfect world, you would end the poisonous relationship you're in right now and stop communicating with this individual. That isn't always useful. It takes a long time to leave an abusive relationship, and occasionally, unfavorable circumstances in life force you to stay in the partnership longer than you would like.

Your life will be much easier when you navigate this tumultuous exit with grey rocking as you make your gradual but steady getaway. Remember that the whole point is emotionally detaching yourself from where you can go.

Grey rocking is a survival strategy used to maintain your sanity while being forced to remain in the presence of an abuser. It is not a way to improve communication in the relationship so that you may continue it.

Grey rock can help you maintain your sanity and reclaim the power that the narcissist has taken from you until you can leave.

It's crucial to understand that it can be very difficult to leave toxic relationships behind if your goal is to distance yourself from the narcissist in order to finally have as little contact as possible.

An abusive relationship requires seven to ten attempts to end on average. Don't be too hard on yourself if you've tried and failed in the past. The best way to permanently leave the company of a narcissist may involve developing and adhering to a long-term escape plan.

The Riptide Method of Ending a Relationship
If you are unable to cut off contact entirely, the Riptide Method is the most effective way to deal with a narcissist you are attempting to leave.

In essence, you are quietly formulating an escape strategy and gradually, little by bit, withdrawing from the relationship until you are finally free of this individual.

The notion that dating a narcissist is akin to being caught in an ocean riptide is the source of the concept. It is deadly, terrifying, and extremely difficult to escape. A riptide can draw you back when you believe you are making headway in breaking free.

Swimming sideways until you progressively approach the shore is the only option to escape a riptide instead of swimming directly toward it. You will handle the narcissist in the same manner.

You will not alert them to any problems because doing so will either: A) cause the narcissist to love to bomb you to return, or B) enable them to try to get rid of you first, which could have disastrous effects on your life, such as trying to force you into homelessness or launching a smear campaign to get you fired from your job.

You might endanger yourself if you warn them, as it would likely exacerbate their abandonment feelings.

So, how does Riptide appear in action? You are gradually removing your belongings from the person if you are living with them. As an illustration, perhaps you store a fresh box in storage or bring it to your parents' house each time you see them. However, you do it in a way that eludes the narcissist.

Locate a Reliable Support Network

A narcissist is not someone you should ever seek help from. But when you are living with someone like this, you require help. Finding out what a good relationship entails is the first step, especially if they are someone you know well and have known for a time. It all comes down to giving and receiving and respecting one another. You give, and they take when you are around a narcissist.

Spend most of your time with people who treat you with honesty, respect, and love. This will assist you in realizing who you are, enabling you to stop needing the narcissist in your life to validate you.

Get started separating from the individual. Because a narcissist craves attention, they frequently attempt to keep people to themselves. This facilitates their ability to exert influence over you. Spend time getting to know new people and reestablishing contact with old acquaintances.

Look for worthwhile ventures and pursuits. Try volunteering, pursuing a new interest, or applying for that promotion you've always wanted. This is a natural support system for you when your life is rewarding.

A Guide to Handling Narcissists

Making the distinction between a grandiose and a weak narcissist should be your first step. When dealing with someone who is vulnerable, you will find that they are hiding their weak inner core under an exterior of self-centeredness and self-absorption. The grandiose people don't hold back when expressing how amazing they think they are and how much they feel like the best.

Behavior from a narcissist negatively impacts your life to treat them with appropriate care. In order to assess them and design the most effective plan, there are several things you need to do to make sure you are handling them appropriately.

Assess the Type of Narcissist

You want to be aware of whether the narcissist you are working with is grandiose or fragile. This allows for determining what is required to elicit their best response. For instance, the grandiose type needs their ego stroking since they believe they are the best. Conversely, because of their brittle ego, the susceptible type is required to always feel unique. They want assurance and praise all the time.

Acknowledge Your Level of Annoyance

Narcissists have a way of getting under your skin, which can make you get irritated with them. They frequently interrupt you when you do anything other than pay them attention because they want all the attention. Don't ignore this at all. Rather, express your annoyance at their behavior so you can begin to stop it.

Examine the Situation

Certain circumstances frequently bring on a narcissist's worst tendencies. Let's say your coworker was vying for a promotion, and someone else was awarded it. If she is a narcissist, she may get extremely insecure and even furious as a result of this rejection. She would thus turn resentful, vengeful, and just plain challenging to work with.

Understand the Cause of the Behaviour

The way a narcissist thinks differs from that of others. Overcoming anxieties is not a particularly difficult task for people who lack narcissism. That's merely a healthy coping mechanism. On the other hand, after experiencing something that made them feel inadequate, a narcissist needs their ego repaired. After a difficult period, it's critical to treat them fairly. When working on a school assignment with a narcissist, for instance, something may happen to reveal a vulnerability in them. You still need their help, even though this may shatter their ego and cause them to quit working on the project. Reassure them in a balanced and necessary way to get them back on track. Approach the problem with this in mind; if you give them too much, their ego will quickly grow too big again.

Don't let the narcissist get the better of you.

If you are doing something that draws their attention away from them, they may attempt to undermine you to persuade you to stop and return to making them the center of attention. Maintaining your focus and not letting anything that people say or do deter you from following your dreams or fulfilling your desires is crucial. For instance, you often spend a Friday night doing something with a narcissist. But you decide that you would want to enroll in a class by yourself. They could attempt to encourage you to drop your class since this diverts your focus from them. Refrain from giving in.

Remember to be optimistic.

Even if they do make you feel horrible, never allow a narcissist to see it since they thrive on seeing other people suffer. Make sure you have a cheerful attitude when you are with them. Keep a grin and ignore their attempts to make you feel bad about yourself.

Make a Bluff Call

It is simpler for them to manipulate you while you remain low, so keep that in mind. Refrain from caving into their negative attempts and try not to take offense. Rather, turn away and/or laugh. If you don't act in such a way in front of them, it begins to diminish their power because they enjoy seeing you unhappy.

They Are Aware That They Need Assistance

One cannot simply take away narcissism as a mental health problem. If they hope to ever manage their behavior, assistance is required. They are unlikely to merely consent and leave if you approach them and suggest they contact a specialist. You could even suggest it, and that could make them defensive or even angry. You will probably need to bring up this topic multiple times before they even entertain the possibility of help. If you truly care about them and want them to at least consider it, approach the topic softly.

Narcissistic Reasons

Though there are a few potential causes, the true cause of NPD is yet unknown. It could be genetics, that the narcissist was raised in an overly sensitive environment, that his parents or other carers modeled manipulative behavior, that the narcissist was abused as a child, that the narcissist had extremely low self-esteem, or that the narcissist's parents used him as a source of their self-esteem. Anomalous brain tissue could potentially be a factor. Acquired narcissism can result from newly discovered fame or fortune.

Narcissism: Overt And Covered

As the name implies, it's simple to spot an overt narcissist. It is obvious how narcissistic he is. He acts haughtily, brags, and expects special treatment. When he receives criticism or feels undervalued, the overt narcissist feels betrayed. He believes he is better than everyone else and hopes to be admired for his actual or imagined abilities. He gets hostile or enraged if his demands are not fulfilled.

In contrast, the covert narcissist is cunning while interacting with others. Even more craftily than the overt narcissist, he gets the devotion he so desperately seeks from others. The covert narcissist may not display outward displays of rage and may come across as modest and caring, yet he is every bit as dangerous and cruel, if not more so.

Insecurities run deep for narcissists, both overt and hidden. Both of them will use deceptive methods to gain approval or recognition. Whereas the covert will employ more passive-aggressive techniques, the overt may employ intimidation to achieve this goal. Neither feels bad about stealing from or demeaning others to achieve their goals. Remember that they are greedy and will take what they desire without offering anything in return. If they give, it's probably so they can receive something in return. These two categories of narcissists are difficult to distinguish from one another, and their traits may even overlap. For example, an overt may also use passive-aggressive tactics, and a covert may fly in a fit of wrath. In general, it is harder to identify a covert narcissist than an overt one.

On the rise

Is the current generation becoming a narcissistic one? Is the prevalence of cosmetic surgery and the proliferation of selfies evidence of this? Between one to thirty-five percent of people are thought to be narcissistic. Since there might be many cases currently undiagnosed, it is still challenging to make an exact determination. Nonetheless, a lot of people think that this generation is all narcissistic.

When it's not detrimental

Everyone possesses narcissistic qualities, which are essential for human growth. Positive traits like self-worth, ambition, confidence, inventiveness, and general wellbeing are the result of healthy narcissism. A person can love others when they have a healthy sense of self-love.

It is believed that narcissistic individuals have more interesting and endearing personalities. Businesses respect narcissists for their self-assurance, initiative, and inventiveness. It is deemed healthy as long as the individual displays the positive parts of narcissism realistically. When the characteristics become exaggerated, fabricated, and abnormal, problems arise. A significant indicator that a person's level of narcissism is unhealthy is relationship failure.

Chapter 5: Self-Obsession and the Narcissistic Mind

Ever wondered what goes through a narcissist's mind? How can someone appear so indifferent to the feelings and needs of others when they are so consumed with their sense of self and importance? Have you ever wondered how someone could construct such a stronghold of obsession with themselves? If so, you're in the correct place because this chapter delves deeply into the narcissist's thinking.

Self-obsession is a typical trait of narcissism, and comprehending it can help us connect to and deal with narcissists more skillfully, as well as provide important insight into their behavior. Understanding the lens that a narcissist views the world through can be the first step toward solving the puzzles of the narcissistic mind. Self-obsession is more than just an inordinate interest in oneself.

What makes comprehending the narcissistic mentality crucial, though? Because narcissists are prevalent in our environment. They could be family members, friends, bosses, lovers, or coworkers. In addition to being enchanting, alluring, and charismatic, they may also be manipulative, destructive, and emotionally taxing. Knowing how they work can be essential to defending our emotional wellbeing and self-defense.

Naturally, this is not a simple route. Entering the narcissist's head can be unsettling and even intimidating. However, I can assure you that if you persevere and maintain an open mind, you will come out on the other side with a far deeper understanding—not only of narcissism but of human nature in general.

What precisely is self-obsession, then? How does it show up in the narcissist's mind? And when we encounter this self-obsession in our day-to-day lives, how do we recognize it and deal with it?

Allow me to guide you through the narcissistic mind's meanderings. We'll go into the world of self-obsession, hoping to learn some surprising things about ourselves.

I want to know if you're prepared to go on this adventure with me before we start. Are you prepared to delve into the darkest corners of human psychology, discover the mysteries of self-obsession, and discover what goes on inside the mind of a narcissist? "The Narcissistic Mind: Understanding Self-Obsession" is the fifth chapter of this journey if your answer is affirmative.

Together, we will go on a voyage of self-discovery and understanding, during which I hope you will find the answers to your questions and the tools and techniques you need to travel your path of self-awareness and personal development successfully. Proceed; the adventure starts now.

After establishing the context for our investigation, we go more into the intricacy of the narcissistic mind. Ever wonder why someone has such a strong obsession with their image? It is essential to comprehend how narcissists see the world through their self-obsession in order to comprehend this. It's a warped perspective that differs greatly from the reality that most of us encounter.

As Sigmund Freud noted in "On Narcissism: An Introduction" (1914), self-obsession is more than just an unhealthy fixation on oneself. It is a mentality in which one's needs and feelings are subordinated to those of others, making one feel like the center of the universe. Narcissists are the main players in this warped view, while everyone else is just an extra or a supporting role in their grand theatrical production of life.

For people who have never experienced this degree of self-centeredness, it can be challenging to comprehend the notion that narcissists regard themselves more than everyone else. When was the last time you felt that you were the most significant person in a situation? Perhaps it happened during a memorable occasion like your graduation or birthday. Imagine now that you feel like this every minute of every day. This is the warped, self-centered world that the narcissist experiences.

In his book "Generation Me: Are We Raising a Generation of Narcissists?" published in 2006, psychologist and author Jean Twenge claims that narcissism is becoming a bigger issue in contemporary culture. In order to function well in a society where narcissists could be our coworkers, superiors, or even our romantic partners, we all need to be aware of this self-obsession.

Comprehending self-obsession also aids in our comprehension of narcissists' seeming lack of empathy. It's not that narcissists lack empathy; rather, it's just that their attention is so focused on themselves that they have trouble thinking about other people's viewpoints. In this instance, the "forest" is their desire and sentiments, and the "trees" are themselves; as the proverb goes, "They can't see the forest for the trees."

Understanding self-obsession can help us better comprehend not only the narcissists in our lives but also our behaviors. Everybody occasionally tends to fall into the self-obsession trap. Does it seem familiar to you to be imprisoned by your anxieties and ideas, unable to see things from anybody else's point of view? If so, you may be a little bit of a self-obsessed person. You're not alone, so don't worry. The first step in conquering self-obsession is realizing that it is a normal aspect of the human experience.

Know What to Know About Mental Illness

We have barely touched on the subject of narcissistic personality disorder in this book. It will be easier for you to avoid getting into a relationship like this if you are more informed about the disease. To attend seminars, read books, do internet searches, and take any other necessary steps to learn as much as possible about this condition.

Develop Mutually Beneficial Relationships

Request assistance

Numerous individuals have gone through experiences similar to yours; therefore, you are not alone. Seek a support network that can provide the necessary resources to maintain equilibrium, stability, and self-assurance in your decisions and progress. Don't hesitate to ask for assistance.

It is not your fault that the person you are in a relationship with doesn't understand their disorder or issue, and even though you were able to support it for a while, you are still capable of recovering and learning how to stop yourself from repeatedly falling into the same patterns.

Assistance is omnipresent and readily accessible. If you cannot attend a public support group or feel uncomfortable discussing it with friends and family, search for other options online. If you wish to keep your identity private, look for an anonymous group to join. Inquire of others about their experiences and the state of their recuperation. Just asking for assistance and letting go of your guilt about your situation will teach you so much.

It only needs awareness and bravery to get rid of the relationship with the narcissist. Any person deserves to be empowered to appreciate life more through a balanced partnership, and you are well on your way to achieving that. By treating yourself with kindness, remaining transparent about your path, routinely processing your emotions, maintaining the high road, seeing the warning signs of a narcissist, and asking for assistance whenever you feel like you need it, you can heal the patterns and ensure that they are broken and cannot be repeated.

You are moving towards becoming the self-assured, content, and well-rounded individual you have always known you are and can be. Although surviving a narcissistic relationship might not seem easy at first, you have all the resources you need to accept your situation and start the healing process.

A one-sided relationship with someone who just thinks about himself is unacceptable. A relationship like this never works out, so it's best to consult a specialist who can assist you in handling situations like these. As they are typically overly possessive, you are usually helpless while dealing with them. They feel that you belong to them; therefore, they emotionally coerce you into continuing in a toxic relationship. Furthermore, they never fail to assign you responsibility for any problems arising in the partnership. They are excellent at assigning blame to a less strong partner. They manipulate your feelings to work against you. That's the reason you feel like you're in prison most of the time. You'll be psychologically coerced into believing that quitting is not an option.

On the other hand, a mental health specialist can assist you in handling the connection appropriately. Walking away might not always be the best course of action. Instead, you can undergo "pro-dependence-oriented" treatment, which will let you stay in the relationship but in a much healthier way. Pro-dependence advocates look at the benefits of residing with challenging individuals and direct our attention towards those benefits rather than vices and the potential misery of maintaining such a relationship. Their strengths have a lot to offer us. They can benefit from us as well. It is possible to make the relationship a mutually beneficial exchange in which you both gain and lose.

Getting a good support group is probably the greatest thing you can do to deal with the fallout from ending your relationship with a narcissist. To learn from the experiences of those who have gone through similar circumstances, you can find a lot of online and offline groups.

It can be simpler to accept that narcissists do exist and that you were never the issue if you know of others who have experienced encounters with them. You can forgive yourself for letting the abuse happen as soon as you accept that narcissists are ultimately responsible for their broken relationships.

Similarly, you may wish to locate someone who can provide context for your emotions. Professionals with expertise in narcissistic abuse therapy may assist you in comprehending your feelings and determining the real reasons behind your narcissistic abuser's actions. These individuals can also provide helpful coping mechanisms and pastimes to expedite and greatly enhance healing.

Not in contact

The impulse to crawl back and apologize may be strong for the first few days or weeks after you've successfully severed the connection. As is often the case with victims, you may feel you have done something wrong and should apologize for your behavior.

Now is the time to remind yourself of your initial reasons for leaving. Remind yourself of the mistreatment and try to see things. Remember the hurt, the rejection, the criticism, and the devaluation, and acknowledge that these were actual experiences you didn't enjoy at all.

At all costs, refrain from placing blame on yourself and stay away from your abuser.

Instead of using the blinds the narc put over your eyes, give yourself the time you need to heal and see the world through clean, unclouded glasses. If necessary, consider putting social media on hold and your phone aside for the moment. Take up a hobby or other activity that will divert your attention from thoughts of your narcissistic abuser.

Is leaving a narcissist usually the right decision?

Rejecting a narcissist can inflict severe narcissistic damage, which is why it is likely to make them feel deeply wounded or furious, regardless of whether it is true or not. When the object of their passion decides they are no longer wanted, a betrayed lover may experience intense pain. A narcissist also experiences intense resentment when someone who provides them with a narcissistic supply—or anybody else, for that matter—decides that they are not "good enough."

Extreme narcissists, who are constantly on guard, could experience rejection for reasons that more typical people would not. It's easy to take it personally when you're too busy or don't have a compelling enough reason to decline their request for your business or participation, which can lead to an unanticipatedly strong reaction. Giving them a valid explanation outside of your control is preferable to letting them know you are rejecting them. It's preferable to say you're too busy to see or see them if your excuse is unarguable, such as when you have to work past your usual hours to achieve a deadline, needs to attend a significant wedding or take a trip or vacation.

Narcissists dislike suffering defeat.

In actuality, they don't. When you declare that your relationship is over, you mean it. However, the narcissist you are speaking with interprets it as an opportunity to go into high narcissistic mode and perceive it as a true challenge, which brings you to:

Narcissists Aim for Triumph

It may appear they are pursuing you, but that is not true. Rather, they aim to restore order and control over the situation, with you abdicating and bearing the brunt of their mistreatment while lavishing them with affection and appreciation. Trust me when I say that there will be consequences for your abandonment if you give in and return. He or she does want you back, but only on their terms and with the same level of narcissism and selfishness that drove you to depart in the first place, if not more.

The goal of narcissists is to constantly monitor you

since he or she is still devoted to you? Not very likely. Honestly speaking, it's likely that they never truly loved you. Their only goal is to ensure that you are in pain and unhappy and will always be so without them in your life.

Knowing that you are genuinely miserable and suffering without them is as fulfilling to a narcissist as persuading you to return to them.

Ultimately, suppose you cannot maintain your focus on your partner throughout the relationship. In that case, they will want to know that you are always thinking about them and having a lot of difficulty while you are apart. He or she will eventually agree to take you back and accept your apology in order to put an end to your pain. Big mistake: the abuse will start over as soon as you are back under their control and won't stop. The greatest reward for a narcissist is control over you, which is what makes them feel most satisfied when you waver between staying with them and going.

Pathological narcissism's effects on productivity and the team

Narcissistic characteristics in a team member or leader can lead to complicated dynamics that are detrimental to cooperation, communication, and the accomplishment of shared objectives.

An effective team can be severely disrupted by pathological narcissism. In an attempt to succeed and take control of circumstances, narcissists often bring attention to themselves. This may result in an unbalanced power dynamic where the narcissist tries to dominate group decisions and actions while assigning other team members to deferential positions.

Narcissists may also find it difficult to collaborate with others and consider other team members' opinions and interests. This self-centeredmindset has the potential to cause division and impair cohesiveness within the group by causing tensions and conflicts. The inability of other team members to feel heard and understood due to the narcissist's lack of empathy can also lead to a less inclusive and more individualized work atmosphere.

Thus, we now know that pathological narcissism hurts teamwork and communication. Narcissists may be less interested in listening to other group members' thoughts and opinions since they tend to concentrate only on themselves. A one-sided communication style where the narcissist dominates conversations and pays little attention to others' input can result from this monopolizing behavior.

The narcissist's lack of empathy impedes genuine and meaningful conversation. Other team members could feel undervalued or ignored since the narcissist doesn't give other people's opinions or viewpoints any thought. This might result in shallow and poor communication, which impedes the sharing of important information and restricts the generation of creative ideas.

The accomplishment of shared objectives and team productivity can both suffer greatly from pathological narcissism. And this can also turn into a big problem for your job! Narcissists may neglect the demands of the team and ongoing initiatives because they are frequently preoccupied with themselves and their goals. This kind of behavior can cause delays in project completion and slow down activities, which will ultimately affect you as well as cause inefficiency and low production.

The narcissist's disputes and tensions might divert your attention and the attention of the entire team from common objectives and issues that require attention. Regretfully, studies indicate that narcissistic team members typically exhibit lower levels of cohesiveness and effectiveness in accomplishing goals. The narcissist's competition and self-centeredness can undermine the group's cohesion and solidarity, making it more difficult for the group to work together productively to accomplish common goals. If you find that you're becoming more aloof from others and that you can't stand them as much as you used to, a narcissist may be working for the organization.

Getting Past Grief

The daughter of a narcissistic mother will go through many stages of grief until she finally learns to let go of her mother. This is a methodical procedure that will assist that daughter in getting over her loss.

Have self-compassion.

You'll have ample time to come to terms with what transpired between you and your narcissistic mother if you are patient with yourself. There is no schedule, so don't set one for yourself. Let the feelings come and go as they want, in truth. We'll talk about mindfulness exercises and strategies later on to assist you in dealing with the barrage of emotions that hits you.

Now, keep in mind that your only goal is to get over your current state of grief. It will take a great deal of patience to do this. You'll experience sadness and self-pity. There is an end to everything that had a beginning, including the sadness and pain you are experiencing. Your sorrow will start, and eventually, it will end and vanish forever.

Recognize when to lower your standards.

You will eventually reach a point where you can acknowledge that the loneliness you are experiencing right now is simply a natural component of the grieving process after being patient with yourself for a while. Along with the other emotions you will experience, such as hate, rage, and regret, sorrow is a natural emotion.

You can now lower your expectations when you've reached the point where you acknowledge the reality that your narcissistic mother showed you very little love and support. Modify your expectations for both yourself and your mother.

Keep in mind that your experience won't be sequential. You won't immediately experience grief, rage, resolve, and a fresh start. That is not how it operates. Eventually, you'll get over your melancholy and turn your life around. One or two triggers may arise when you try something new, like a new professional route.

Your memories are triggered by them, which makes you experience worry and anguish once more. You may occasionally ask yourself, "I thought I was over this?"

Once more, lower your standards. Things like that have a way of coming back to bite you. You should prepare for the return of all the hurt, rage, and grief that you now anticipate.

Locate your haven, which could be a fortress of seclusion inside your head or the company of friends. Mental toughness can be accumulated and developed, but it will take time. It takes us right back to step 1: practice self-compassion. Additionally, keep in mind that these steps are not linear. You can go directly to the next stage and return whenever necessary.

Acknowledge all that you are unable to alter.

Once more, you can go straight from step 3 to step 1 or even step 2. This phase can be moved at any point during the process. Once more, there is no right or wrong way to go about processing your loss.

Nonetheless, accepting the things in your life that you cannot alter is essential in learning how to get over grief. This is a crucial step.

If you're the daughter of a narcissistic mother, you could think you have no control over anything. You believe that you are powerless over most things or even that you are powerless over anything at all.

Naturally, that is untrue. Many areas of your life are within your control and subject to your choice. It's up to you to decide not to become upset when someone calls you names. It is your decision which person to believe in. Even what you wear on your upcoming date is up to you. You can select the color of lipstick you wish to wear.

But as soon as you accept power over something, you must accept the things you cannot alter. For instance, you have to come to terms with the fact that you cannot alter your mother. She might already be out of reach, no matter how much good you do, how much you forgive, and how much you try to reach out to her. You may not be able to persuade her to make the required adjustment.

Fixing and gluing together the proverbial broken mirror is a pointless endeavor. You might even cut yourself during the procedure. The picture you see in the mirror is already damaged and won't ever be whole again, even if you can glue all the parts back together.

Look for the good in others.

My brother and my paternal grandma gave me the strength to accept that I could not change my mother and that I had to move on with my life. Without them, I doubt I would have been able to do so.

My brother was the only one who, for the longest time, saw our mother for the violent narcissist that she was. Our father is still living in denial. Despite my brother's best efforts to persuade me otherwise, I believed I could change our mother. He never lost up on me, and when I did eventually turn around, he got me out of there and provided housing for me.

My paternal grandmother became the mother I never had after that. She consoled us both, believing my brother and me when we told her about our mother and even believing us over her son. She provided us with a haven where we could go to process the emotional wounds our mother had inflicted on us. And these are only two of the countless friends and relatives who supported me through this difficult time.

Isolating their victims is one of the strategies employed by abusers—we have previously discussed this before. In actuality, you are cut off from any possible network of support that you might have had during the abuse.

Anyone who truly cares can offer you the much-needed assistance you require. All you need is for them to show that they care enough to listen to you; they don't even need to say anything. Though it could seem like you're using them as a sounding board, that's not asking for much.

A buddy willing to listen to you more than a relative or a church pastor more eager to vent to you will be of greater assistance to you. They are genuinely lending you their strength when they listen to you, even if it's just a tiny bit of it.

Small or large, the strength you derive from their understanding and forbearance will make a big difference. They don't have to be individuals who have experienced the same thing as you; as long as they are empathetic, everything will work out.

How to Support a Narcissistic Husband in Chapter 6

You might be able to confront your spouse with the reality. Alternatively, assist them in confronting and overcoming their narcissism. In order to accomplish this, you must first assist them in identifying and releasing themselves from the self-aggrandizing and self-demeaning ideas trapped inside their mentality. The values and personalities they had developed since they were young children. These attitudes towards themselves and others must be changed.

The narcissistic spouse must go one step further and set themselves apart from any undesirable characteristics held by their parents or early carers. They may exhibit some of these characteristics in their own life. These characteristics could include an arrogant "I'm better than everyone" or a condescending "I'm good for nothing" attitude. In order to protect themselves from any neglect, abandonment, or both that they may have experienced from their parents or carers, they must also acknowledge and give up any self-created attitudes that they may have absorbed. Originally designed as survival strategies, these self-made attitudes have now been ingrained in their subconscious as the standard way of life. Additionally, they must eliminate their tendency to be conceited and overbearing and think of others as inferior. They must overcome the constant desire to evaluate themselves against other people.

The next step in the process is to support the partner in prioritizing self-compassion over self-esteem. Being cognizant of one's unpleasant elements, treating oneself with kindness, and acknowledging one's shared humanity are all aspects of self-compassion. While self-esteem emphasizes the urge to be unique and centers on how you compare to others, self-compassion combats the tendency towards narcissism that can arise from a concentration on self-esteem. To treat other people and living things as distinct entities and separate beings as they are, one must possess self-compassion. Seeing one's flaws and "defects" is another benefit of practicing self-compassion. They say, "A problem is half solved once recognized."

But it's important to remember that empathy is only the pants in the narcissist's emotional closet—it's not absent. You must assist them in locating and extracting it. A narcissist will only become more defensive and thick-skinned as a result of criticism or name-calling. We must be gentle with them if we want to help them and are confident they will accept our assistance.

The narcissistic spouse needs to acknowledge and overcome their negative and self-centeredbehaviors in order for the process to start and finish. They must reject notions that make them feel superior and self-aggrandizing.

They start focusing on donating and showing generosity to those in their immediate vicinity. This will eventually assist them in turning their attention away from themselves by increasing their empathy and care for others.

Many studies have been conducted on many levels regarding the best ways to assist narcissists in overcoming their undesirable tendencies, and the majority of them come to the same conclusion: kindness and empathy. They feel more confident and willing to open up if we use these two approaches. They usually grow more devoted to the partnership and more loving. They must be made aware of how crucial these connections are. They cannot change their characteristics by being ignored or blocked by their relationships, but they can learn to be compassionate towards themselves. Using comforting and encouraging words is quite relevant, as is reminding them of the value of the partnership. We must be gentle with them and let them know how we truly feel—without patronizing. They are encouraged to consider the relationships and change their focus from "me" to "us" by this kind of reassurance. They need to know we can provide "secure love."

It is important to acknowledge that while this method might work for those with narcissistic features, it might not work for those with chronic narcissistic personality disorder (NPD), and those with complete NPD might not be able to recover.

When we gently and righteously offer assistance, people typically give it a second thought. However, there's a danger that if they reject your strategy, they won't accept your assistance in general.

When your narcissistic spouse truly apologizes, tries to change certain patterns of behavior, becomes less self-centered, and shows concern for your well-being.

Nevertheless, not all narcissists are open to change. Instead, they would prefer to merely deny that they require assistance. It will be difficult for them to recognize the requirement as they cannot own up to any form of flaw or error. No matter how minor or major the issues are, some people find it impossible to accept they have them because of their extreme guilt, fear, and dislike of even the tiniest bit of criticism. Through self-persuasion, they believe they are perfect in their current state. It is not seen to be an option for them to relive the feelings of rejection, hurt, and embarrassment they experienced as children.

Options for Treatment

The most beneficial assistance for a narcissist is expert assistance. Simple home remedies won't be able to quickly improve this mental health issue. Treatment is necessary for a narcissist to stop their harmful behaviors. Although there may not be a cure, treatments are available to help them build deeper connections.

Psychoanalysis

Psychotherapy is the most effective treatment for narcissistic personality disorder. Therapy sessions are required alone, in groups, or with the family. The intention is to assist the narcissist in comprehending the reasons behind his actions and convictions. Therapy also teaches children how to interact with people productively.

Empathy is a necessary skill for understanding other people, and narcissists lack it. Is it something that can be taught? Research indicates that it can. This is beneficial for narcissists since treatment sessions focused on empathy may teach them to be understanding of other people's viewpoints and experiences.

Pathological narcissists may learn to accept accountability for their decisions and deeds with a significant amount of therapy. It might also help kids develop the ability to set reasonable goals. Narcissists know how to establish and preserve healthy interpersonal connections.

The Narcissistic Mind's Inner Workings

The main query you're undoubtedly itching to know the answer to is: Just how precisely do narcissists influence their victims? Research has indicated that individuals diagnosed with pathological narcissism or narcissistic personality disorder have some degree of neurobiological impairment, albeit there isn't a single, definitive explanation for this. This makes a lot of sense, given that psychopathy includes NPD. Ten years ago, researchers studied the brain patterns of people diagnosed with pathological narcissism using neuroimaging as part of a study on the disorder. They discovered that people with NPD had less gray matter in the parts of their brains that control empathy, which is consistent with the findings of the earlier study. These scientific investigations have produced sufficient data to conclude that individuals with

NPD have a reduced ability to participate fully in society. It's even possible to argue that individuals with NPD suffer from abnormal brain functioning that prevents them from forming fulfilling relationships with others.

The anterior insular cortex, a part of the brain linked to empathy, is problematic for those with NPD, according to different new neuroscience research. Although narcissists' victims will probably characterize them as "bad people," this isn't always the truth because narcissists' behaviors and actions are sometimes inadvertent because they are unable to control their symptoms. This indicates that it is not intentional and that they are unaware of the harm they are causing; it does not imply that what they do is good. This chapter will cover malignant narcissism, victim selection techniques used by narcissists, manipulation techniques, and the symptoms of narcissism in those in positions of power.

How Do People Get Manipulated by Narcissists? Should you have previously encountered narcissism, you might already be familiar with the tactics your abuser employs. The tactics used by all narcissists to maintain control over their victims while also preventing them from leaving are essentially the same. A balance must be struck to keep their prey encircled around their finger. Narcissists employ a wide range of strategies to pervert their victims' perceptions of reality and place the blame on them rather than on themselves. These strategies are employed by others who may not be narcissists as well, but narcissists use them excessively. Let's examine the tactics that are most frequently employed.

Conditioning

Narcissists typically succeed in getting you to prioritize them and give them your full attention. They will try to make you identify your positive experiences, skills, and attributes with mistreatment, annoyance, and anger. They accomplish this by subtly disparaging or insulting your positive attributes. They might even attempt to undermine your objectives or spoil get-togethers with family and friends. To make it difficult for you to escape the abusive situation, some narcissists even go so far as to isolate you from your friends and family and attempt to make you financially reliant on them. They instill a fear of performing the activities you once found enjoyable. Narcissists act in this way because they want all of your attention to be focused solely on them. They will try to lessen the possibility that anything outside your life could endanger their authority over you. In addition, pathologically jealous narcissists desire nothing and nobody else to ever stand in the way of your relationship with them. The most detrimental kind of conditioning is experienced by those whom narcissistic parents raised. Since you don't know any difference, you are readily shaped and conditioned when you are a child.

Mental Tricks

Narcissists are unlikely to engage in deep and contemplative dialogue since they will almost certainly engage in numerous psychological tricks to enhance their perception of themselves. Projecting, gaslighting, and having circular talks are common techniques used by narcissists to divert your attention, divert your focus, and persuade you to agree with their viewpoints. This tactic is intended to make you feel horrible for being a regular person with genuine opinions that could differ from theirs and to confuse, irritate, and discredit you to divert attention from the underlying issues. A narcissist would have you to blame if there was an issue. If you've had discussions with a narcissist, you should be aware that they invariably conclude with you questioning how the disagreement got started in the first place.

You likely disagreed with them about something absurd, like the color purple in the ocean. Your life, profession, decisions, friends, and family are attacked. All of this occurred only because their inflated confidence and feelings of self-worth were damaged by your disagreement, leading to a narcissistic injury.

Gaslighting

Whether or not they are aware of narcissists, many individuals are familiar with the term "gaslighting." Common statements like "Are you crazy?" and "You just imagined that" or "That never happened!" can be used to depict gaslighting. A person's sense of reality can be undermined and distorted through gaslighting. It will keep you from accepting the abuse and mistreatment and rob you of your ability to believe in yourself. When a narcissist is gaslighting you, you can find yourself doing the same to bridge any cognitive dissonance you may be experiencing. Let's say that you have been gaslighted by your narcissistic abuser for a while. If that's the case, it starts to undermine your confidence in yourself, leading you to conclude that whatever they say is true and your senses are probably faulty or that you require their validation to validate your ideas. You must reaffirm your beliefs to your support network, document events as they occur, and ground yourself in reality in order to withstand and recover from gaslighting. Regaining your sense of reality and your ability to lead yourself again can be greatly aided by having a strong support system.

In charge

Narcissists have an insatiable drive to be in charge in all situations. They'll attempt to control your money and social media and keep you apart from your loved ones. They will essentially try to micromanage every part of your life. For this reason, narcissists will fabricate conflicts out of the blue to upset you.

They will argue over little matters and become enraged if they perceive any slight against them. You will be less able to trust your judgment and reality about the abuse you are experiencing and the more control a narcissist has over your feelings.

Calling someone names

A narcissist's final option when using manipulative techniques is typically to call someone names. This is typically employed when they have run out of other strategies to control your behavior or viewpoints. To them, calling you names is a simple and fast way to minimize you, make fun of your intelligence, and put you down. Name-calling is frequently employed to disparage its targets' perceptions, ideas, and convictions. A well-informed and well-researched viewpoint wouldn't guarantee that the narcissist wouldn't twist it to make you feel foolish. If they cannot persuade you otherwise, they will go after you directly and try to discredit your credibility and intelligence. When name-calling occurs, it is crucial to stop the conversation immediately because it is unlikely to progress and could even worsen your sentiments and confidence.

What Is and Is Not Possible

Never do narcissists accept responsibility!

Their self-perception is characterized by perfection or worthlessness, and they are rarely, if ever, willing to accept accountability for their actions. To them, taking ownership of their mistakes and responsibility for them amounts to acknowledging their flaws and worthlessness. If they do take responsibility, it destroys their self-worth and triggers their self-loathing problems. They also believe you will detest them because they are "flawed," that belief only makes them feel worse.

Do you recall the dispute about tidying the kitchen before the movie started? To resume, your narcissistic partner is feeling happier.

You're not allowing them to get near you and hug you good morning. You inform your friend that the dispute caused the evening to be destroyed. Instead of making them wait and view the movie first, they turn the tables and accuse you of being the one who cleaned up the kitchen. And thus, the debate starts anew with these radically divergent points of view.

As you now know, narcissists never say sorry or accept responsibility because it would be too embarrassing for them to do so. Having stated that, even if they are aware of their error, they most likely won't apologize. You shouldn't anticipate an apology—at least not spoken.

Offering sweet offerings, such as bringing you to your favorite restaurant or buying a surprise gift, is the equivalent of an apology to a narcissist. This is a reparative gesture; accept it and let go of the desire for an apology if you want peace and the relationship to move past the disagreement.

Decide which fights to engage in. You have to learn to let go of inadvertent slights that come your way. If you keep telling your egotistical partner when they offend you and cause you pain, the relationship will eventually end with you and your partner fighting all the time.

Even though it would be so much easier to talk things out rather than argue, arguments should occur when significant and purposeful insults are directed at you that go beyond boundaries that you will stand by if you decide to leave and stop the relationship.

Be ready to abandon the relationship and walk away if your narcissist disregards your limits and won't accept responsibility for their actions.

Recall that your narcissist will say and do anything they want if you allow them to, so be sure to correct them if you don't catch them doing it.

Narcissists are not interested in talking about or processing past disputes. If you want to talk about your most recent argument, what went wrong, and how to handle a disagreement better the next time, your narcissist will not even entertain the idea. They believe you're criticizing them and not genuinely attempting to resolve your disagreements as a pair, only to remind them of their inappropriate behavior.

Use the pronoun "we" while talking about your previous interactions to try and succeed in finding a better approach to disagree. Singling out their actions and using the word "you" to express disapproval of them simply fuels an egotistical and inflammatory mental process.

Protect The Limits You've Selected To Establish

The boundaries of other individuals are never noticed or respected by narcissists. Your narcissist will feel free to say and do anything they wants without thinking twice about respecting you or your feelings if you don't decide to be clear about what constitutes bad narcissistic behavior and draw the line between what is acceptable and unacceptable behavior.

Narcissists have no problem openly criticizing your family, your style of dress, your choice in music and movies, your opinions (if they differ from their own), and everything else you can think of. They will do it by calling names and making disparaging comments. Many of their comments and taunts will be light blows in an argument. After saying ugly things, they will pretend that nothing happened and there was never an argument.

For some narcissists, making embarrassing public spectacles doesn't bother them. Some narcissists take great pleasure in humiliating situations that occur in public. They may do anything from storming out of a busy restaurant because they don't appreciate how long it takes someone to take their order to yell loudly, fight, and overtalk you as you attempt to get a word in.

Once a narcissist exhibits any of these behaviors, they will likely do so repeatedly. This is how they interpret the affront to their self-worth and how they respond to that interpretation.

This is the point at which you must determine your boundaries and where to draw the line. If they engage in what you consider to be the most reprehensible behavior, you must make it plain that their actions are unacceptable. If they still don't respect you and your boundaries, be ready to call it quits.

After verbal abuse escalates into physical abuse, your relationship with a narcissist should quit. It would be wise to break up with your narcissistic partner right away unless you enjoy getting hit and kicked and do not set boundaries about the verbal abuse they inflict on you.

If you don't establish boundaries in your relationship, it may start quietly with a friendly arm hold or a painful pinch.

It is never easy to be in a relationship with a narcissist, especially when it involves a significant other. But, if you choose to stay in the relationship, it will go much more smoothly if you know what to expect from a narcissist and how they think and respond.

Establish boundaries and protect them with steadfastness. If you can draw the line with a narcissist, you should be able to withstand NPD.

#: You Prefer a Shift-Reaction Compared to a Support-Reaction

Shift responses are conversational strategies that turn the attention of your discussion partner to you. In contrast, a support response keeps the focus of the conversation on the other person by asking questions.

Consider a scenario in which you are conversing with individual A. You will not ask person A any questions when they say, "I want to buy a phone," since you are a narcissist. You won't likely respond with, "Yeah? Do you have a certain name or brand in mind?

Rather, you will bring up your newly purchased Samsung Galaxy S20 Ultra. You will discuss how wonderful it is, how much it costs, and how "rich" person A must be to purchase it. One of the main characteristics of narcissism is this talkative style. If you observe that you have this propensity, be more mindful of it and get a diagnosis.

Adopting a shift response makes you want to put yourself first in every conversation to take advantage of the chance to highlight your special or noteworthy qualities. You listen for signs that you can use to turn the conversation around to you, rather than listening to hear and comprehend what others are saying and using that to establish a connection.

Observe how you converse with family, friends, and coworkers to determine if you favor the shift response. You have narcissistic tendencies if you can't go five minutes without thinking about when someone will respond to you in a conversation or intentionally draw attention to yourself.

#: You're in a magical place.

When it comes to themselves, narcissists are never as amazing as they think they are. They typically have low self-esteem. As a result, individuals frequently inhabit a fantasy-driven mental realm where they can balance their grandiose illusions with the fact that they are flawed people!

You may have narcissistic tendencies if you frequently tell yourself stories about how amazing, wealthy, successful, attractive, or handsome you are, even while you are none of these things. If you frequently exalt and inflate your intelligence, prosperity, strength, beauty, or attractiveness, you've established a fantasy universe in which these things exist. This insight ought to prompt you to get a professional diagnosis.

In order to shield their delicate egos and to get the outside approval and validation they so desperately need because they feel inadequate on the inside, narcissists frequently construct fantastical worlds. If you identify as a narcissist, your defensive response to criticism and viewpoints that challenge your brittle sense of self is a result of your wooing of this fantastical world.

#: You Want Recognition And Appreciation

The fragile ego of narcissists collapses when they receive no appreciation, acknowledgment, or accolades. Because of this, if you are narcissistic, you probably want more from your relationship than just sincere praise. Rather, you will probably want a steady supply of affirmations from your partner or coworkers because your fragile ego and self-image depend on it.

As was previously mentioned, narcissists dislike criticism and opposing viewpoints, particularly when they run counter to the fantastical world they have constructed. Their best company is that of YES men and women, who are generous with their praise and compliments due to this indifference.

You recognize treachery when any YES men or women in your immediate vicinity stop being forthright with their praise and compliments. This response is frequently hostile or coercive, intended to force the other person to give you what you want—affirmation!

#: Insufficient Empathy

Empathy deficiency is another characteristic that narcissistic people frequently exhibit. The capacity to comprehend and relate to the thoughts, feelings, and perspectives of others is known as empathy. This skill is absent in narcissists.

If you are narcissistic, on the other hand, your main focus will always be on your demands and how you can satisfy them. Developing healthy relationships is difficult because of their lack of empathy, relentless need to always get their way, and the self-centeredness they encourage.

Narcissists never hesitate to take advantage of others to accomplish their desired goals because they are insensitive to the feelings of others. Your main focus will be on achieving your goals (your manner). As a result, you will regard the important individuals in your life as interchangeable parts on a cheeseboard.

Moreover, you will typically be unaware of the negative impacts of your words and deeds on others since you will feel admirable and superior to them. Rather, you will frequently think that others are fortunate to have the opportunity to assist you in achieving your goals and being in your life, partly due to a lack of empathy. This idea will cause tension in your relationships with people you intentionally harm or who you deceive into thinking you are someone deserving of worship.

In addition to being self-centered, narcissists also tend to be control freaks who want to be in charge of everything. This implies that you will get hopeless or point the finger at others when things don't turn out how you hoped. Additionally, when things don't go your way, you'll become intolerant of opposing viewpoints and indifferent to the psychological and emotional needs of others, which will result in angry outbursts.

If you are a narcissist, you will frequently use deceitful tactics to achieve your goals in order to safeguard your fantasy world and self-image. For example, you might denigrate, mock, or even attack the individual expressing criticism or a viewpoint that goes against your notion of yourself as unique.

Use the criteria we've provided here to assess yourself as honestly as possible to identify narcissistic behavior. Seek a professional opinion or diagnosis if many of these behaviors and character traits are present in your personality.

Let's talk about the reasons for this personality disorder before moving on to how you can quit being a narcissist or overcome narcissistic behavior.

Chapter 4: Well-Being Narcissistic

Without learning more about the current theories around so-called "healthy narcissism," it is impossible to begin to comprehend the personality disorder known as NPD. Everyone should be happy with who they are and strive for success. Living with a bad self-image and lacking confidence makes succeeding difficult, particularly in our competitive, free-market economy. The psychological theory known as object relations is the source of this notion of healthy narcissism.

Everybody Is An Object In Somebody's Subconscious

The theory goes that adults relate to other people because of how they interacted with their parents when they were young. In their subconscious, memories of how they were handled as babies become "objects." When adults are reminded of their parents by others, their subconscious anticipates that individual's behavior toward them. The subconscious will predict a response consistent with the memory if the object triggers memories of abuse or neglect or positive experiences and nurture. Consequently, this theory "born" the idea that individuals are considered like things because the items that "live" in the subconscious developed during infancy and early childhood. A person's family and social interactions are greatly impacted by their subconscious ability to foresee how others will treat them.

A Good Relationship With Subconscious Objects And Consequently With Others In Life A healthy narcissist will have subconscious objects that help them behave appropriately toward those with whom they have relationships. This enables the healthy narcissist to have rewarding interactions with others and to give and receive satisfying interactions. Healthy subconscious objects do not have to be treated as something to be utilized only for accomplishment and self-aggrandizement;

rather, they support the development of a genuine self-image that is in balance with the ego.

The Root Causes Of Pathological Self-Centering

It is said that when a person struggles to love the things that are buried in their subconscious, narcissism is toxic and pathological. The ensuing frustration is said to give rise to an obsession with self-love and subsequent megalomania.

Section Five

Making Every Effort To Avoid Narcissism

Avoid Using Severe Parenting Styles

Seek to prevent or at least lessen the risk of narcissistic personality disorder (NPD) in newborns and early children by looking to the parents and/or primary caregivers. The consensus is that NPD results from the way that newborns and early children are raised, despite some equivocal data suggesting that there may be genetic and psychobiological components that contribute to the illness. Males appear to be more vulnerable to NPD than females due to the "macho male" culture in which we live, although girls are also at risk and can develop NPD throughout adulthood.

Teaching People That It's Alright to Feel and Express Vulnerability When It's Appropriate

When parents show disapproval when their kids act needy or display fear, they may be setting the stage for their child to grow up to be a narcissist. Instead of stifling every need or fear, parents should educate their kids on effectively communicating their vulnerability to the right people at the right times for the right reasons.

Abuse and Neglect

The worst parenting transgressions that foster an environment conducive to adult narcissism include never expressing affection, abusing children emotionally or physically, and neglecting them. These circumstances may have disastrous effects.

Accomplishments and Recognition

Additionally, giving children praise and rewards should be suitable for the situation. A young child's growing personality can be harmed by receiving too much praise, especially if it is undeserved, by giving in to misbehavior, or by receiving no praise.

Can I Trust My Parents?

Allowing a child to receive uneven care is another parenting error. The last thing children need to learn, especially when they are young, is that their parents or other key caregivers are possibly unreliable and won't always be there when they need them. The young person must be able to reasonably anticipate that their needs will be satisfied promptly.

The Parent Who Is Too Macho

Last but not least, it appears that some of the most skilled narcissistic manipulators pick up these techniques from their parents. If parents use manipulative tactics to get what they want from their kids, they are probably teaching their kids these "skills" and putting themselves in a position where they will manipulate them in the future. They also expose their kids to manipulative behavior from other people, like teachers, potential spouses, coworkers, and even their kids.

The Culture And Narcissism

"Me Decade"

Were you alive in the 1970s and 1980s already? If so, you might recall that, despite indications of what would come in the Seventies, the Eighties were specifically dubbed the "Me Decade." Consumer satisfaction was the main theme of the advertisements. The customer was and still is adamant about obtaining what he desires.

Ads today essentially function in the same way. There are a lot of arguments in favor of the notion that you will become better, stronger, more attractive, and so on. Examples are "This product will make you work less" and "This will make you look better than the rest." The narcissistic self is driven to betterment.

You'll see that narcissism is stronger and making a comeback in popular society these days. Narcissists are becoming so prevalent that they are even occupying prominent roles. Why is this the case?

Stars

Consider the most evident: celebrities. Their lifestyles are currently even more visible to the general public. Through social media, they can connect with a larger number of fans. The way celebrities display themselves used to exude refinement and mystery. They will only appear in ten-minute interviews or motion pictures. They might walk into award presentations and strike a photo for the cameras. It's completely different now. Celebrity communication gets more involved. Admiration intensifies as followers watch their live videos on social media or personal websites and their reality TV series. It extends beyond advertising. In their narcissism, celebrities think—and rightfully so—that their lives are so significant that they should be turned into successful businesses. Not just perfume manufacturers but also celebrities are honored with perfume names. Fans desire to smell like their idols. The list of examples is endless.

Social Context/Business Culture

A fresh form of narcissism is on the rise. It's the kind that's encouraged and embraced. This contemporary idea of self-glorification is believed to be the opposite of socialism. It eliminates the person's desire to maintain a social connection. Brotherhood and cooperation are things that the narcissist has no interest in. In this world of greed and power, he is more concerned with bettering himself and his needs.

Additionally, narcissism is starting to be seen in a somewhat good way. It is believed to be a form of self-defense against aggression rather than an extreme, warped form of self-love. Sigmund Freud thought that narcissism is essential. Freud is more intrigued by the relationships between narcissism and the wellbeing of the id and ego. This contrasts with Erich Fromm's willingness to accept any local explanation, particularly the one that separates narcissism from socialism.

Regardless of what psychoanalysts may say, narcissism is starting to negatively impact the mental health of both narcissists and those who support them. The example from a few lines ago is that the fan is the facilitator, and the star is the narcissist. The fan is completely engrossed in the celebrity's stronger personality in this powerful relationship. Some fans might even begin to disassociate from their heroes and consider themselves a reflection of them. To deal with the reality that they are not as well-liked or affluent as the people they are admiring, they may grow into their unique form of narcissism. Therefore, they may give in to the alluring delusion of the narcissist's world.

Sociology versus Psychology

If the psychology of narcissism is your area of interest, you will be studying one person or at least several examples of the same kind of person. However, sociology focuses more on studying a group or a culture. Although the chapter examines how narcissism is becoming increasingly socially acceptable, each person's experience with it is unique.

Nonetheless, sociology has an impact on narcissism. Narcissism is more likely to grow in societies that value the individual above the community or individuality over communalism. However, while there may still be some narcissists in cooperative communities, the majority of them are more understanding of the needs of others. A narcissist, on the other hand, is entirely concerned with his well. Historian CristopherLasch attributes the dissolution of the once strong bonds between family and community members to "market forces" and "cultural progressivism."

Self-Progression and Self-Preservation as a Survival Strategy

Many people nowadays have to choose between their survival and that of others. Most of the time, you can't hold them responsible. People must eat. People need to ensure their survival.

Here are some scenarios that require careful examination:

Mr. Smith is employed by a corporation that has a bad reputation. Strong ties to the government mean this allegedly corrupt corporation is unlikely to close anytime soon. This company offers many benefits. Some have quit the company due to moral judgment and personal values. To remove the dishonest head, some people have staged protests. Mr. Smith will not participate in any such demonstration. His well-paying job is one he wants to keep.

On her social media accounts, Denise shares multiple photos of herself. Every image shows the same locations. Usually, her face is enhanced and even filtered to make it appear even better. The likes she receives bring in money for her. For a charge, she even gets to endorse items. Family and friends advise her to change jobs due to the negative feedback she has been receiving. Denise doesn't give a damn about what people think. She navigates life far more smoothly than most people do. She settles her other debts and rent.

The Al Fresco neighborhood is holding a book drive. The goal of the book drive is to gather as many books from the local families as possible. The books will be given to houses and public schools that don't have many books. The Peters family knows about the book drive, but their hectic schedules prevent them from participating. Not a single member has chosen to remove books from their piled-high shelves. Their business is not the book drive. They are not immediately impacted by it.

Emil arrives home ahead of the rest of the family. He uses this as an opening to reach for the tub of ice cream. Emil has declared first dibs on the entire amount of ice cream, even though there is still enough for the entire family. He feels he should have it because he is the only one at home. The fact that his sister loves strawberries and asked their mother for them doesn't bother him.

It is a hypochondriac, Mrs. Shelley. She gets sick every time her kids want to take a vacation somewhere. She's going to want to throw up. She'll feel lightheaded. She occasionally even says she has a temperature but hasn't checked with a thermometer. Even if she doesn't have a condition, she wants her kids to stay with her and care for her.

Which of the following, in your opinion—after reading this—is a true narcissist? You're right when you state that making judgments based on a single event in one's life can be challenging. Still, you can already begin to speculate about which ones—whether or not they are narcissists—are the worst.

In the first instance, Mr. Smith's work attitude is the only topic of discussion. Perhaps this is merely an instance of self-preservation. Being very self-centered or self-preserving can be confused with narcissism. Mr. Smith will prioritize himself and his family over other people; that much is certain.

It could be the same thing as the second case. Denise is merely at work. But there's also a further level of laziness and selfishness here. She doesn't care if other people think she's shallow, which is sometimes good. She is ignoring her family's legitimate concern, though, that she has selected a profession requiring little talent and little responsibility. There will be an issue with this later on.

The Peters family lacks empathy and sympathy for others in the third scenario. Their problems are the only things that fascinate them. Nothing beyond their home's four walls can force them to go beyond what's comfortable. Perhaps the Peters family is ordinary. It might even be the perfect family. The issue with this is that it's a great environment for rearing narcissists in children. The connections with the community at large have been severed. The kids imitate their parents' actions. When someone is more than capable of helping others, showing little concern for them has been appropriate.

The fourth example, Emil, might be a young narcissist in the making. Perhaps he sees this as sheer wickedness. It can be perceived as selfishness by his parents. On the other hand, it might be concerning when there is a disregard for other family members. Emil could very well be headed towards being a cold-blooded narcissist if his parents don't intervene.

Mrs. Shelley appears to be a fairly decent illustration of a subliminal narcissist in the final and fifth examples. The term "hypochondriac" here indicates that her behavior is ingrained. Here is an illustration of a complete narcissist. She does not, however, truly fit the cultural and contemporary notion of what a narcissist acts and looks like because of how sad she appears. Narcissism is encouraged in society by roles such as bossy boss, political achiever, showy celebrity, diva vocalist, and so on. A contributing factor to this spreading disease is the comfort-seeking customer. While Mrs. Shelley is a narcissist, she is not the type that this chapter addresses.

Chapter 3: Strategies for Narcissistic Manipulation

Given that manipulation is a prevalent indicator of narcissism and behavior frequently employed by narcissists, you must get a comprehensive understanding of manipulation. First of all, a narcissist can transform into any type of manipulator they so choose. It frequently depends on what the individual hopes to get out of the circumstance.

The theater is one kind of manipulator. As previously mentioned, a narcissist will frequently threaten them, in part because it's a potent kind of manipulation. You may have frequently heard your mother threaten to physically harm you if you disobeyed her. She may have threatened to stop loving you if you didn't comply with her requests. A narcissistic mother will employ a range of threats to harm her child.

Although most parents occasionally threaten their children, it's crucial to remember that a narcissist will escalate these threats. A normal parent, for instance, would never threaten to stop loving their child if they don't follow their rules. The only hazard here is from a narcissistic parent. Most parents show their children unconditional love and would never consider telling them they didn't love them just because they didn't follow their instructions. Most parents anticipate that their child would occasionally defy them or refuse to comply with their requests immediately.

But a narcissistic parent does not anticipate this because, well, that is just how a narcissist thinks. She expects her child to listen to her whenever she asks them to do something. A narcissist, particularly one who asks her daughter to do something for her, feels so important that there is no excuse not to comply with her requests.

The guilt tripper is a second kind of manipulation. Narcissists use this kind of manipulation to manipulate you into believing them or doing something. The narcissist will be able to guilt you no matter how hard you try to stop feeling guilty, convincing you that you are the worst person alive and that you don't care about them. The person can shame you into thinking that you are the one who is uninterested in him, not him. So why should she care about you if you don't care about her, as a narcissist would think? To put it another way, a narcissist would frequently employ the guilt tripper as a manipulative technique to make you feel guilty about something.

Competing is the third manipulation tactic a narcissist would employ. A narcissist will take this to a different level, even while most parents would frequently utilize a little bit of competition between their kids to get things done, like cleaning the rooms or seeing who can get to the car the fastest. Furthermore, in order to obtain what she wants from you, a narcissist is more prone to use various types of manipulation in a competitive setting. She might say, for instance, that you don't love her enough if you don't get a scholarship. Most of the time, you have no full control over this. For example, even if you put in the most effort, you might not be awarded the scholarship because the committee decided that someone else was a better candidate. But the fact that you lost indicates that you didn't show your mother enough love. Put another way, you don't love your mother enough if you lose a competition because you didn't give it your all for her. This is an illustration of how a narcissist would approach competition: by taking things too far.

Conversely, your mother may have frequently competed with you to outdo you. She may have asked you to play a game, race, or participate in an activity she is skilled at. She would then talk down to you when you lost to her, telling you that you weren't intelligent or strong enough to prevail. She could also convince you you can never defeat her since she is always superior. But if you ever succeeded, you will probably face her fury. She could, for instance, accuse you of cheating and punish you accordingly. She may also try to make you feel guilty about coming out on top.

Attacks on your self-esteem by a narcissist are the fourth sort of manipulation. This is one of the most popular ways a narcissist manipulates others because it's how she usually makes herself feel superior to everyone else. She can defend herself if she can discredit you for whatever. A narcissist is aware that in order to make you appear less dangerous, she must undermine your self-worth.

The main issue with this kind of manipulation is that your mother doesn't seem to care how much it bothers you. This is frequently the result of her trying to emotionally and psychologically destroy you so that, even if you are superior to her in some area, you won't think you could ever excel in anything. Of course, the harm caused by poor self-esteem is greater than most individuals realize.

The use of quiet treatment is the fifth method of manipulation. It is practically a given that a child may occasionally give her parent the silent treatment, particularly during her adolescent years, but this is not a widespread occurrence unless the parent is a narcissist who frequently manipulates others to achieve her goals. For instance, like most teens do, once you hit adolescence, you most likely begin to question your mother's narcissistic tendencies. You still pushed your mother, even though you might have been more circumspect about what and how you challenged her to avoid upsetting her. Naturally, a narcissist will not take any kind of challenge well and would soon resort to manipulation to get rid of it as quickly as possible. The silent treatment may be one of these strategies, particularly if you've already responded to this coercion.

When your mother employed the "silent treatment," she would avoid contact in any way, regardless of whether you asked for or needed her assistance. Indeed, in certain cases, a parent applying the silent treatment will not even look at her child. Naturally, this is just another deceptive ploy to accomplish her goals and make you feel awful about what you did. She employs this tactic and other sorts of manipulation to instill dread in you. It's an attempt to show you what she can do if you ever challenge her again.

www.ingramcontent.com/pod-product-compliance
Lightning Source LLC
Chambersburg PA
CBHW052152110526
44591CB00012B/1949